ANIMAL LIFE STORIES

THE WHALE

Published in 1989 by Warwick Press,
387 Park Avenue South, New York, N.Y. 10016.
First published in this edition by
Kingfisher Books, 1989. Some of the illustrations
in this book are taken from the First Look
at Nature series.

6 5 4 3 2 1

Printed in Spain

Library of Congress Catalog Card No. 89-50009
ISBN 0-531-19062-5

ANIMAL LIFE STORIES
THE WHALE

By Angela Royston
Illustrated by Jim Channel

Warwick Press
New York/London/Toronto/Sydney
1989

The blue whale plunges into the orange-colored
water and takes a vast gulp. She squeezes the soupy
water through her huge baleen plates. Then she
swallows the tiny krill caught in them. Suddenly
there is a movement near her and a hungry killer
whale glides by.

The blue whale knows he will not attack her. She is too big for him. The penguins see him coming, and squawking with fear, they jump from the water onto the ice. But the killer whale dives under an ice floe and tips it up. With a loud splash an unlucky penguin falls into the sea.

All summer, the blue whale has been feeding in the cold Antarctic, and a thick layer of blubber has built up under her skin. Now, as winter comes and the sea turns to ice, she starts her long journey toward warmer waters.

Every few minutes she comes to the surface and blows out a blast of air. A plume of mist rises over the sea. She breathes in deeply and sinks downward again. One day the whale hears a strange and lovely sound. A group of humpback whales are all singing their high-pitched song. She passes them and swims farther and farther on until the water slowly gets warmer.

Three months later she reaches the subtropical sea. She floats in the water feeling its warmth all over her body. But there is little food for her here, as the plankton she feeds on live mainly in cold water.

One day she senses another blue whale nearby. She
calls out and a big male swims close to her. He
swims around her and touches her with his snout.
They rub against each other and soon they mate.

Two months pass and the whale is thinner now and
hungry. It is time to return to the Antarctic. As she
swims she makes a stream of clicking sounds. She
can tell from their echoes whether a rock or ship is
nearby. One day she swims close to a rocky outcrop.
A humpback whale is scraping off the barnacles
that cling to its body.

At last she is back in cold waters again. She finds a shoal of plankton and gulps in mouthful after mouthful of the tiny krill. As she feeds she hears a young blue whale crying out in terror. A pack of killer whales is swimming around the calf, biting it. Quickly the big blue whale goes to help, lashing the killer whales with her tail. Another blue whale comes to help and they drive the pack away.

The months pass and winter comes again. Some whales stay behind in the cold water, but the blue whale swims back to the warmth. All this time a baby has been growing inside her, and she knows it will soon be born.

When the calf is born it slithers out tail first. The mother nuzzles his warm body and pushes him up to the surface of the water. He grunts and squeals as he takes his first breath of air and starts to swim, helped by his mother.

Unlike his mother, the newborn calf has no blubber. He needs to feed right away. He finds his mother's nipple and drinks her warm milk. At first he spends most of his time feeding. He grows fast and is soon twice as heavy as when he was born.

The weeks pass. The calf still stays close to his mother, but now he loves to swim around her and flop onto her back. He stretches his head out of the water, then twists around and dives under her body. They call and sing to each other as they swim.

One day the mother and calf hear the thrashing and thrusting of water deep below them. A sperm whale is fighting with a giant squid.

The squid grasps the whale with its huge tentacles.
The whale writhes but cannot loosen the squid's
hold. Then she gets her teeth into the squid, and
soon the battle is over. The sperm whale swallows
her meal and comes to the surface, panting for air.

The calf is now five months old, and his mother is very hungry. They set off for the Antarctic. The calf still feeds on his mother's milk, but when they reach the cold waters she teaches him how to catch krill.

The calf grows fast and a thick layer of blubber forms beneath his skin. Soon he is big enough to look after himself. In autumn they will return to warmer waters and his mother will mate again.

More about Whales

The blue whale is the largest animal that has ever lived. An adult is as long as three buses put end to end and weighs as much as 14 buses. These vast animals eat krill, which are about the size of shrimp.

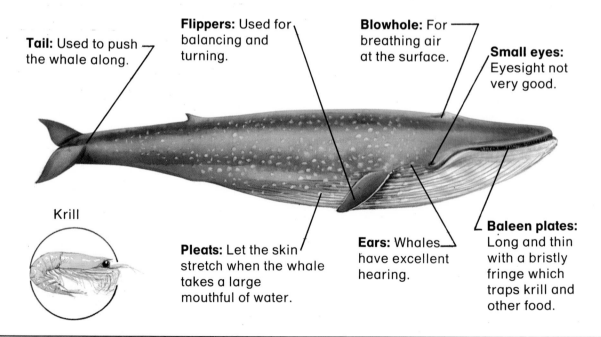

Tail: Used to push the whale along.

Flippers: Used for balancing and turning.

Blowhole: For breathing air at the surface.

Small eyes: Eyesight not very good.

Krill

Pleats: Let the skin stretch when the whale takes a large mouthful of water.

Ears: Whales have excellent hearing.

Baleen plates: Long and thin with a bristly fringe which traps krill and other food.

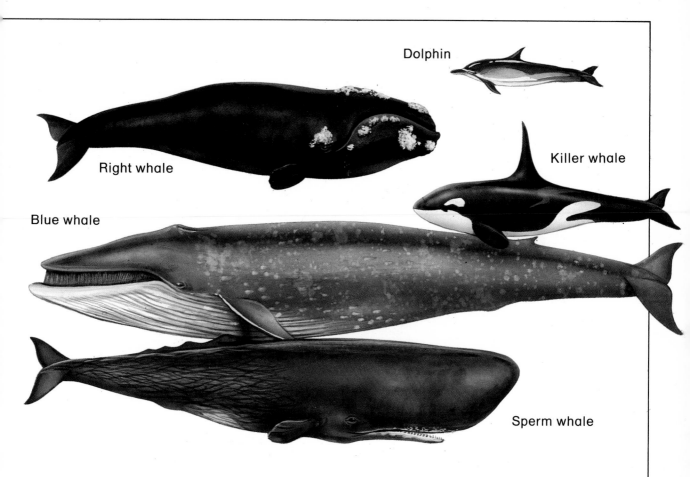

Dolphin

Killer whale

Right whale

Blue whale

Sperm whale

There are two main kinds of whales. Blue whales, right whales, and humpback whales are all baleen whales. They feed on shoals of krill and other plankton. Sperm whales, killer whales, and dolphins are toothed whales. They eat small fish, but killer whales attack penguins, seals, and other whales.

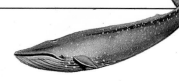

Some Special Words

Antarctic Cold lands and ocean around the South Pole.

Barnacles Small shellfish which cling to and grow on rocks, ships and some kinds of whales.

Blubber Layer of fat which keeps the whale warm. The layer is thickest after the whale has been feeding all summer and thinnest after the whale has not eaten anything for a long time.

Giant squid Large deep-sea animal with long tentacles.

Plankton Tiny plants and animals that float on the sea. Most are too small to see with your eyes. Blue whales mainly eat krill, which are a kind of animal plankton.

Shoal A group of fish or sea animals.

Subtropical waters The warm seas near the equator.